To My
Wonderful Father,
from Your
Loving Daughter

With all My
Soul...
Donna

D1300571

Other books by

Blue Mountain Press INC.

Books by Susan Polis Schutz:

Come Into the Mountains, Dear Friend
I Want to Laugh, I Want to Cry
Someone Else to Love
Yours If You Ask
Love, Live and Share
Find Happiness in Everything You Do
Don't Be Afraid to Love
To My Daughter with Love
on the Important Things in Life
Take Charge of Your Body
by Susan Polis Schutz and
Katherine F. Carson, M.D.

Warmed by Love
by Leonard Nimoy

I'm on the Way to a Brighter Day
by Douglas Richards

Anthologies:

With You There and Me Here
Reach Out for Your Dreams
I Promise You My Love
A Mother's Love
A Friend Forever
You Are Always My Friend
It Isn't Always Easy
My Sister, My Friend
Thoughts of Love
Thoughts of You, My Friend
You Mean So Much to Me
Love Isn't Always Easy
Don't Ever Give Up Your Dreams
When I Think About You, My Friend
I Love You, Dad
I Keep Falling in Love with You
I Will Always Remember You
For You, My Daughter
A Lasting Friendship
I Will Love You
Through Love's Difficult Times
Always Follow Your Dreams
Though We Are Apart, Love Unites Us
Mother, I Love You Forever
I'll Be Here When You Need Me
The Best Thing in Life Is a Friend
Creeds to Live By, Dreams to Follow
Thinking of You, My Sister
My Dream Is You
Mother, Thank You for All Your Love

To My
Wonderful Father,
from Your
Loving Daughter

A collection of poems
Edited by Susan Polis Schutz

Blue Mountain Press ™

Boulder, Colorado

Copyright ©Stephen Schutz and Susan Polis Schutz, 1988.
Copyright © Blue Mountain Arts, Inc., 1988.

All rights reserved. No part of this book may be reproduced in any manner whatsoever
without written permission from the publisher.

Library of Congress Catalog Card Number: 87-63561
ISBN: 0-88396-261-6

ACKNOWLEDGMENTS appear on page 62.

Manufactured in the United States of America
First printing: February, 1988

Blue Mountain Press INC.

P.O. Box 4549, Boulder, Colorado 80306

CONTENTS

To My Father
from Your Daughter

For all the years I can recall,
you have always been there for me.
You guided me with wisdom and patience,
then stood back and watched me grow.
I realize now how difficult
    it must have been
to stand in the background as I made
    my own mistakes,
but you never turned away.
You trusted that I would make the
    right decisions
and find my own direction.
Thank you for your never-ending
    faith in me.
I love you more than any words can
express, and I want you to know
how very proud I will always be
to call you my father.

— Dana O'Donnell

This Is for You, Dad

This is for you,
for the father I love,
for the one who has cared all these
years, but has never heard enough
    about how much I care.

So this is for you.
For the one who has
helped me through all my childhood
    fears and failures,
and turned all that he could
    into successes and dreams.

For the man who is a
wonderful example of what
    more men should be.

For the person whose
    devotion to his family
is marked by gentle
    strength and guidance,
and whose love of life,
    sense of direction,
and down-to-earth wisdom
make more sense to me now
than nearly any other thing
    I've learned.

If you never knew how much
    I respected you, I want
    you to know it now.

And if you never knew how much
    I admire you. . .let me just say
    that I think you're the best father
    that any child ever had.

        This is filled with love.
        And it's all for you, Dad.

                                    — Adrian Rogers

I May Not Still Be Your Little Girl, Dad, but I'll Always Love You Just the Same

Dad, I may no longer be that little girl
who always wanted another hug
or another minute with you,
but I still miss you when we are apart
and long to spend more time with you.

I may no longer need your hand for
every step I take,
but I still need your acceptance
and support of everything I do.

I may not be that little girl who asked
for all the things she ever wanted
in the world,
but that's because long ago,
you taught me how to go after my dreams,
and to trust you to give me praise
and encouragement every step of the way.

I may no longer be that little girl
   who looked to you to share every
   hurt, smile, and tear,
but I still feel like her whenever
   I think of you —
the most caring, loving father
      in the world.

I'll always love you, Dad,
   with the heart of that little girl
grown to love you only more.

— Carol Maatta Oberg

Dad, You Will Always
Be Home to Me

There are few doors in my life that I can enter without first knocking — carrying no gift, no invitation, just myself — and feel the immediacy of a genuine welcome. Home has always been one.

There are few people in my life who have seen me at my very worst and my very best — whom I can be with or away from, yet have no fear of being hastily judged or unfairly criticized. You have always been one.

There are few times in my life when I have told you what you mean to me, though I often believe you already know. But I want this to be one of those times.

For all the comforts of home, the generous constancy of your love, you are held warmly in my thoughts, close in my heart, and always with love and affection.

— Carol Ann Oberg

As Your Daughter, I'll Always Appreciate and Respect You, Dad

Dad, it is not always easy
to tell you how I feel about you.
I have left many of my thoughts unspoken,
thinking there would be another time,
a better time, to talk,
and yet, time keeps passing by,
and it makes me realize
that the time is now
to let you know
how thankful I am for your love.
I appreciate you and respect you, Dad,
and though I don't tell you often,
I certainly feel it in my heart
always.
I love you.

— Deanna Beisser

A Daughter's Wish
for the World's Best Father

This is my wish:

That in your life,
    which is so precious to me,
may troubles, worries, and problems
never linger; may they only make you
that much stronger and able and wise.

And may you rise each day with sunlight
in your heart, success in your path,
answers to your prayers, and that smile
    — that I love to see —
        always there . . . in your eyes.

— Carey Martin

I Don't Tell You Enough, Dad,
but Thanks for Everything

So many days go by
without our letting the ones
we care about most
know just how much we appreciate them.
Too many days and too many
opportunities have already gone by, Dad,
but please know how much I love you,
need you, and care about you.
Not just for the things you
have given me,
but for the examples you've set,
the values you've taught me to live by,
and the support you've always given,
even when I deserved it the least.
Thanks, Dad.
I love you very much.

— Laurie A. Napoleone

For Dad, for Always
from Your Little Girl

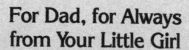

I love your smile, your laugh,
   your love of life.
I respect your wisdom, though
   in my naive youth
many times I doubted it.
I admire your strength, your
   courage,
and I hope that I have inherited
   a small part of it.
For all you've given me, for all
   you've taught me

through times of pain and times
   of joy,
I could not love you more; and yet
each time we talk, each time
   we are together,
I am certain that I have never
   loved you as much as then
and not nearly as much as I do now . . .
   for always, Dad.

— Coleen Robinson

My Father . . .

Sometimes you used to let me
   fall down,
just so I'd learn how to climb
   back up again.
Sometimes you would try to keep
   me from doing something
because you knew I'd be hurt,
but I'd do it and hurt myself
      anyway.
Sometimes you were away
   when I needed you,
but I always knew you'd come home
   soon.
Sometimes you cried because
   you were so proud of me,
and sometimes I cry
      because I love you
         so much.
      Always, I'm thinking of you . . .

— Jean E. Attebury

Always Remember, Dad,
How Very Much I Love You

Dad,
you've always been here
to want me;
to love me and take care of me;
to teach me and to mold me,
not as you were or wanted me to be,
but as I chose to be;
to understand when I try
for everything the world has to offer;
and to be patient
with my recognition
of your love.

I learn more each day
about life and living,
but my most valuable lesson
is realizing how important
you are in my life,
how much you have given me,
how much I have taken,
and how little I have shown
    my appreciation.

For everything you have done,
always remember
how very much I love you.

— Brenda Check

Dear Dad . . .

I want you to know
that even though
my feelings somehow
  don't get spoken
       like they should . . .

the feelings are always
  warmly here,
    in my heart, for you.

And they would love
  to thank you
  for everything
     you are to me . . .

for everything you have done,
and for every wonderful thing
you continue to do.

You're really something, Dad.

— Adrian Rogers

Being Your Daughter, Dad, Gives Me So Much Happiness

I'm happy today
and almost every day.
My life is good,
and so much of that
is due to you.
I was thinking
about this today,
and I realized
that I really want
to thank you.

You've given me
so much.
You've given me
the self-confidence
to know that
I can be exactly
what I want to be
and the strength necessary
to attain those goals.

You've given me support
in those times
when things aren't going
as exactly as I planned.
You've given me the courage
to pick myself up
after those low times.

You've given me
principles and guidelines
by which to live,
and yet,
you've given me
the freedom
to choose my own path.

I've always known that
no matter what happens,
you've always been there
standing right beside me,
giving me the strength
to face life head-on.

And I've always known
that no matter who I become,
you'll always love me,
just as I
will always love you.

— Patty Wiener

Dad, You Always Have
My Love and Appreciation

Dad, you have always been
such a strong influence
in my life.

I have always looked to you
for approval and admiration.

You have been beside me
through everything
I have done.

And because I always wanted
you to be proud of me,
I have strived to do my best
and to become the person
that I am today.

— Christine Anne Keller

You're the Kind of Father
Every Daughter Wishes For

Dad, you're the kind of father every
    daughter longs for . . .
You've given me a firm foundation
    of faith
and taught me the importance of
    honesty in my life.
Because of that, I will always
    respect you.

Though our family has had hard times,
you've been a source of strength on
    which I can depend.
Yet, you've never been ashamed to
    reveal your weaknesses
or too proud to admit your mistakes.
That only reinforces my admiration
    for you.

But most important . . .
you've shown me the meaning of love,
always encouraging me to be the best
    that I can be.
Even when I fail or disappoint you,
your love never fails.

Thank you, Dad, for all you've done
    and all you've been to me.

— Susan Ellington

With Thanks, Dad, from Your Loving Daughter

Dad, your life is full of giving,
and it's not very often
that you ask for anything in return.
You're too concerned about
the rest of us
to worry about yourself.
You're always there when we need you.
When we don't know where to turn,
we turn to you.

Your strength never falters;
your love enfolds all of us.
It's nice to know
that in our uncertain lives,
your love is the one thing
we can be sure of.
Thanks for being there, Dad.

— Judy Bourgeault

No Daughter Could Have
a Better Dad than You

If I could have
chosen the man
to be my dad,
I would have chosen a man
who put family above all else,
a man who worked hard,
yet had a gentle touch
   and an easy smile.

I would have looked for a man
who never asked others to do
what he would not,
but who set an example
with his own life and values
that others would want to follow;
a man who could admit mistakes,
find the courage to learn from them,
and keep going forward.

I would have chosen a humble man,
one who was close to nature
and respected all living things;
a man who was content with life
and found joy in the smallest things.

If I could have chosen the man to
be my dad,
I would have chosen a man
of integrity, honor, and love.

I would have chosen no one
    but you, Dad,
for you are all these things.

— Bettie Meschler

Thank You, Dad

You have mended my broken toys, my
broken dreams, and my broken heart,
and put them all back together with
love, patience, and understanding.
You were always ready to help, to talk,
or just to listen.
And even when I caused you worry or
heartache, I could see the love in
your eyes and know that it would always
be there, no matter what I did.
You gave me the timeless gifts of
solid values and belief in myself
and my abilities.
Thank you for all this and more,
and most of all —
thank you for your love.

— M. Joye

Dad, I'll Always Appreciate
Being Your Daughter

As a child, I walked in your presence.
In your presence I felt warmth,
the security of love;
I felt safe, protected from all harm.
In your presence I felt happiness;
everything seemed better with you there.
I felt complete and content,
with no need to worry about tomorrow.
You filled my childhood with all
     the securities
I needed to grow into adulthood.

As an adult, I'm proud to walk in
     your presence.
You taught me to give to others,
     to love without question,
to share, to give to others who have less.
You taught me to laugh at myself
and let others laugh with me;
     to be honest, for I have no need
          to be anyone but myself.

You taught me that working for something
can give me pride in myself;
to be sensitive to others, for
everyone has a right to their feelings.
You taught me to enjoy the world,
to love, respect, and touch people and nature.
You, Dad, have given me
all these gifts . . .
giving them to others is my gift to you.
I love you, Dad, and I
  feel so proud to be your daughter.

— Susan M. Cain

To My Dad

I remember the times
when you would tell me
how proud you were
of the things I'd done.
I can still hear
your encouraging words
and sometimes your words
of caution.
But I wanted you to know
that I'm the one who is proud
of having a dad like you —
someone who believes in trying
and always gives his best.
Thank you for being there for me.

— Deanna Beisser

Thank You, Father,
for Your Constant Love
Throughout the Years

Through the many changes in my life,
you have stood by me when you could
and let me go my own way
when you couldn't do anything else.

You struggled to help me do
the right thing
and suffered with me when I didn't.
My joy has always been yours,
and my happiness your true goal.

If I had been wiser,
I would have taken your advice
more often and without argument,
but you let me be me.

I have made my own mistakes,
but your love has always
   brought me back.

I am full of appreciation
   for your love,
your wisdom,
and your never-failing belief in me.

I love you dearly.

— Lonnie Browne Zangrillo

Dad, I Love You
Just for Who You Are

Dad,
when I was little,
I loved you simply
because I was your daughter
and you were my father;
it was an emotion
that was just always there,
as long as I could remember.

Now, I am an adult,
and I've seen you
as a person,
someone human,
just like everyone else.

It comes with time,
learning that a parent
can't, and shouldn't,
be perfect,
and that parents, too,
have dreams, goals,
and even fears.

And now I've learned
that I love you
not only because you're my father,
but also just for who you are.

— Jacqueline R. Kenny

A Daughter's Memories of You, Dad

I look beyond today
at the many gifts of strength
that are truly memories of you, Dad.

The trials and burdens
you had to bear,
time spent
teaching us how to tie our shoes,
how to ride our first bicycles,
participating in our sporting events.
You were always there.

Many times
I remember saying:
 Dad can do it!
 Dad can fix it!
 Dad's so smart!
 Dad can do anything!

I look beyond today
at that shoulder I always leaned on
and I realize the many gifts of
strength that are truly memories
of you, Dad.

— Rala J. Mahdi

There's So Much
I Want to Say, Dad

There's so much I want to say to you,
so many "thank-yous" for the things
   you've done.
I can't remember a time when
   I asked for your help
that you didn't give all of yourself.
Life seems to get so busy at times
   that we often forget
the love that binds us.
But I wanted to tell you
   that I haven't forgotten.
I appreciate you for being there for me,
   and I love you, Dad.

— Deborah Uva

Dad, I'll Never Forget
Everything You've Done for Me

Dad, I have been thinking about you
a lot lately,
and I am beginning to realize how much
you have done for me.
There were times when I failed to see it,
and there were years that I didn't show you
the gratitude you deserved,
but I know now that I couldn't have been
given a better parent than you.

I hope you never blamed yourself
      for any of my mistakes
and that you never questioned your abilities
      as a parent.
I put you through some trying times,
but you never gave up on me,
      and you never withdrew your caring.
And that is one of the many reasons that
I'm going to try to erase the mistakes
      I have made
and replace them with the love
      I should have shown long ago
            for you.

— Ann Rudacille

From Deep Within My Heart
Comes My Wish for You, Father

I could never repay your commitment
   to my life
by expressing my gratitude with
   any amount of words,
but only with the deep love and respect
   held for you within my heart.
You have been so much a part of any decision,
   both conscious and not,
that I have ever made.
And though you may have thought
that all those years of advice and ideas
   you gave me
just slipped through me without a pause,
I can honestly say that those values
   are now so greatly used
in my search for myself.

You are one of the greatest
    and most guiding forces in my life,
and no matter how high your expectations
    of me may be,
I promise that I will make you proud of me.
I may not always be right in my choices,
but I may not always be able
    to take chances,
and for now I must follow my heart.
My father . . .
words can be arranged in any number
    of beautiful ways,
but none are so beautiful as those
    spoken from the heart,
and these have come from deep
    within mine —
        I love you.

                                — Cathy MacDonald

Dad, You're So
Important to My Life

It's not unusual for
daughters to have a difficult time
telling their fathers
  how important they are
    and how much they are loved.

I know that I am sometimes
    that way with you, Dad.

I can talk with you about
    so many things; we reminisce
    about the times of our lives.
We talk about how things are going
    with me, with our family, with our world.
And I try to keep you in touch with
    the things that are going on in my life.

But of all the things I say to you,
I know that I never share
    this message enough

    . . . that you're such a very
        important part of my life, Dad . . .

        and I love you.

— Carey Martin

Fathers and Daughters
Share a Bond Forever

Over the course
of my lifetime,
I can't count the times
I had the chance
to tell you
how much you mean to me . . .
and I let them slip by
to wait until another day.
But Dad,
I don't want to wait
to tell you
how much I love you . . .
There are times
even now
when I want to wrap my arms
around your neck
and crawl up in your lap,

and have you comfort me
even though I'm grown.
And there are times
when I reach
for the phone,
knowing your voice
will pull me through
my dark moment,
because I know you're there
for me in this world of uncertainty . . .
and you love me regardless . . .
for who I am
and for what we are —
    a part of each other forever.

— Sandra Mayhew

I'm So Glad
You're My Father

You and I are family.

And no matter what else happens
in this sometimes
    crazy world of ours,
I want you to know, Dad . . .

I'll always be here for you.
I'll be thinking of you, like
    I always do; thanking you
    with all my heart for being
        the special person you are to me.
And I'll be here
        in whatever way I can be . . .

    cherishing you,
        feeling proud and happy for you,
            and caring about you
                forever.

— Collin McCarty

Dad, Even When We're Apart, You're in My Thoughts

I can't always be there with you
like I want to be.
But my thoughts will
find their way to your side,
and in my mind we'll be together,
sharing our memories and laughter.
The one thing that distance
will never change
is the closeness of our hearts
or my warmth of feelings for you.

— Edmund O'Neill

Dad, I've Always Been Proud to Be Your Daughter

It's never been easy for me
to try and find the perfect words
to say how I feel about you.
Yet, even though
the words aren't said,
I hope you know how much
you mean to me.
Since there are no perfect words
to describe how I feel about you,
I'll just say what's in my heart,
and that, Dad, is "I love you."

— Shirley Oneschuk

"I love you, Dad"

What can you say
to someone who has
always been one of
the most essential parts of your world;
someone who took you by the hand
   when you were little
and helped to show the way?

What do you say to someone
who stood by to help you grow,
providing love, strength and support
so you could become the person
   you are today?

What can you say to let him know
that he's the best there is,
and that you hope you've inherited
    some of his wisdom and his strength?

What words would you say
    if you ever got the chance?

    Maybe you just say
            "I love you, Dad . . ."

    and hope he understands.

                    — Andrew Tawney

ACKNOWLEDGMENTS

We gratefully acknowledge the permission granted by the following authors to reprint their works.

Jean E. Attebury for "My Father . . ." Copyright © Jean E. Attebury, 1983. All rights reserved. Reprinted by permission.

Brenda Check for "Always Remember, Dad, How Very Much I Love You." Copyright © Brenda Check, 1988. All rights reserved. Reprinted by permission.

Patty Wiener for "Being Your Daughter, Dad, Gives Me So Much Happiness." Copyright © Patty Wiener, 1988. All rights reserved. Reprinted by permission.

Christine Anne Keller for "Dad, You Always Have My Love and Appreciation." Copyright © Christine Anne Keller, 1988. All rights reserved. Reprinted by permission.

Bettie Meschler for "No Daughter Could Have a Better Dad than You." Copyright © Bettie Meschler, 1988. All rights reserved. Reprinted by permission.

Jacqueline R. Kenny for "Dad, I Love You Just for Who You Are." Copyright © Jacqueline R. Kenny, 1988. All rights reserved. Reprinted by permission.

Deborah Uva for "There's So Much I Want to Say, Dad." Copyright © Deborah Uva, 1988. All rights reserved. Reprinted by permission.

Ann Rudacille for "Dad, I'll Never Forget Everything You've Done For Me." Copyright © Ann Rudacille, 1988. All rights reserved. Reprinted by permission.

Deanna Beisser for "To My Dad." Copyright © Deanna Beisser, 1988. All rights reserved. Reprinted by permission.

Susan M. Cain for "Dad, I'll Always Appreciate Being Your Daughter." Copyright © Susan M. Cain, 1988. All rights reserved. Reprinted by permission.

M. Joye for "Thank You, Dad." Copyright © M. Joye, 1988. All rights reserved. Reprinted by permission.

Rala J. Mahdi for "A Daughter's Memories of You, Dad." Copyright © Rala J. Mahdi, 1988. All rights reserved. Reprinted by permission.

A careful effort has been made to trace the ownership of poems used in this anthology in order to obtain permission to reprint copyrighted materials and to give proper credit to the copyright owners.

If any error or omission has occurred, it is completely inadvertent, and we would like to make corrections in future editions provided that written notification is made to the publisher: BLUE MOUNTAIN PRESS, INC., P.O. Box 4549, Boulder, Colorado 80306.

This book is printed on fine quality, laid embossed, 80 lb. paper. This paper has been specially produced to be acid free (neutral pH) and contains no groundwood or unbleached pulp. It conforms with all of the requirements of the American National Standards Institute, Inc., so as to ensure that this book will last and be enjoyed by future generations.